A MORE PERFECT [

A More Perfect [

Jimmy McInnes

BookThug 2015

 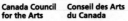 

Canada Council **Conseil des Arts**
for the Arts **du Canada**

ONTARIO ARTS COUNCIL
CONSEIL DES ARTS DE L'ONTARIO
an Ontario government agency
un organisme du gouvernement de l'Ontario

The production of this book was made possible through the generous
assistance of the Canada Council for the Arts and the Ontario Arts
Council.

LIBRARY AND ARCHIVES CANADA
CATALOGUING IN PUBLICATION

Library and Archives Canada Cataloguing in Publication

McInnes, Jimmy, author
        A more perfect [/ Jimmy McInnes.

Poems.
Issued in print and electronic formats.
ISBN 978-1-77166-096-9 (PBK.). – ISBN 978-1-77166-116-4 (HTML)

        I. Title.

PS8625.I525M67 2015   C811.6   C2015-900800-X
                                        C2015-900801-8

PRINTED IN CANADA

In memory of Jack

[Begin Speech With]

Name of municipality. Name of state, province, or region. Name of month. Name of date of month. Name of year. All Gregorian.

[As Prepared for Delivery]

Begin speech with relevant historical quotation:

> quote plural pronoun definite article collective plural noun comma preposition verb idiom preposition verb indefinite article comparative adverb adjective noun period endquote

State how long ago these words were spoken. State exactly where they were spoken and the proximity to where we are now. Give a veiled idea of how many people were there. Gender these people who were there when these words were spoken.

Highlight the ease with which any collection of words is spoken and then contrast that ease with the potential impact that words could have on a country's political ideology.

Allude to an engagement between the working class and the information class; allude to an engagement between the political class and a transcending term for those who love their country. Make mention that these groups had all congregated to where these words were spoken when these words were spoken for similar reasons these words were spoken and reference the specific legislative action that was taken following these words being spoken.

Be sure to highlight that the legislative action that was taken following these words being spoken was indeed a physical action and not merely a theoretical one.

Provide a disclaimer to the above statement that the physical action taken to fulfill the theoretical action remained in itself an incomplete action.

Remind the audience that [unanimously hated act of racial subjugation] not only delayed the physical and theoretical action that was taken following these words being spoken, but that also [unanimously hated act of racial subjugation] was fundamentally connected to the history of [relevant nation].

Make sure to note that the issue of [unanimously hated act of racial subjugation] was a particularly controversial one that divided [relevant nation] on geographic lines.

Make sure to note that the issue of [unanimously hated act of racial subjugation] divided those present when these words were spoken to the extent that the physical action taken to fulfill the theoretical action remained in itself an incomplete action with regard to [unanimously hated act of racial subjugation] for an approximate amount of time after these words were spoken.

Note that those present when these words were spoken chose a general term for a group of people to be born at a later date as the adequate party to take theoretical and physical action regarding [unanimously hated act of racial subjugation] as it pertained to legislative action.

Beginning with the use of an idiom:

> Assure the audience that the theoretical action for
> [unanimously hated act of racial subjugation] was something
> fundamental to the physical action taken after these words
> were spoken.

Exclaim that the action taken after these words were spoken had essentially contained an ideal regarding the nature of fairness under an organized judicial system.

Add that the action taken after the words being spoken contained the following attributes:

> 1) Had promised freedom from arbitrary or despotic control.
>
> 2) Had contained the moral principle determining just conduct.
>
> 3) Had defined the terms for a group of political bodies with
> the ability and need to become the concept of the ideal over the
> progress of [an unspecified number of dates].

Interject this list of favourable characteristics regarding the theoretical action taken after these words being spoken by highlighting the fact that the theoretical action taken after these words being spoken was insufficient in materializing as a physical action regarding [unanimously hated act of racial subjugation].

Clarify in the second clause of this sentence that the theoretical action taken after these words being spoken should have, but failed to, apply in full to two of the genders included in all racial groups and all religious affiliations actively associated with [relevant nation].

Emphasize that the burden regarding [unanimously hated act of racial subjugation] had to be shifted to those who came after these words being spoken.

Divert mid-phrase in order to reinforce this point by providing broad examples.

Divert mid-phrase in order to reinforce this point by providing spatial examples.

Divert mid-phrase in order to reinforce this point by providing historical examples.

Underscore that those who came after these words being spoken stood to lose short-term in pursuing the above examples.

Now return to your original point, highlighting that those who came after these words being spoken remain with the burden of the disconnect between theory and practice of the action taken after the words were spoken in their particular historical context.

Bridge a connection between the action that was taken following the aforementioned words being spoken and the current historical moment as it pertains to those present.

Clarify that this has always been a policy objective of great importance.

Dramatize this connection between the action that was taken following the aforementioned words being spoken and the current historical moment as it pertains to those present by using a physical metaphor.

Emphasize that the physical metaphor you are using is helpful in articulating the goal of achieving [list of abstract ideals] for [relevant nation].

Transition now from the collective-we to the first-person-I while still emphasizing that your current status as a candidate for [relevant office] stems from a need for the collective-we.

Make the point that all contrasts inherent in the collective-we are derived merely from one's own personal narrative.

Confront these differences by emphasizing a list of similar personal aspirations.

Continue to flesh out this point by highlighting obvious differences of appearance and location.

Drive this point home by returning to the physical metaphor as it pertains to the need for the collective-we.

Articulate that the physical metaphor symbolizes improved conditions for one's own kin at a later date.

State that your optimism is grounded in the confidence that [list of flattering qualities] can be attributed to the citizens of [relevant nation].

Use this last statement as a springboard to reintroduce your own first-person narrative and how it pertains to the goals of the collective-we.

[Pause for applause]

[Contextualize Your Person]

Contextualize your person in relation to your father, his race, and his country of origin.

Contextualize your person in relation to your mother, her race, and her state of origin.

Contextualize your person in relation to your grandfather, his race, the economic circumstances of his day, and his history of military service.

Contextualize your person in relation to your grandmother, her race, and her place of employment during your grandfather's history of military service.

Contextualize your person in relation to the quality of your domestic education.

Contextualize your person in relation to the economic situations of the various countries in which you have had residence.

Contextualize your person in relation to your spouse, her race, and the curious duality regarding [unanimously hated act of racial subjugation] apparent in her genealogy.

Contextualize your person in relation to your daughters, an adjective describing their value, and their relation to the curious duality regarding [unanimously hated act of racial subjugation] apparent in your spouse's genealogy.

Contextualize your person in relation to various immediate and extended family members, their race, their skin tone, and the amount of locations they can be found around the globe.

Contextualize your person in relation to your life's duration, the strength of your memory, and the probability of your personal narrative occurring in other nations as opposed to [relevant nation].

Contextualize your personal narrative by acknowledging that your personal narrative is unprecedented when compared to the history of candidates for [relevant office].

Contextualize your personal narrative by stating that your personal narrative has internalized the notion that [relevant nation] depends upon the collective-we.

Contextualize your personal narrative by providing a common phrase that illustrates the notion that [relevant nation] depends upon the collective-we.

Contextualize your personal narrative by reiterating the notion that [relevant nation] depends on the collective-we by providing a second common phrase.

Contextualize your message as it pertains to the last approximately three hundred and sixty-five days.

Contextualize your message in relation to the commentator's evaluations regarding the people of [relevant nation].

Contextualize your message in relation to the commentator's evaluations regarding the perceived market value for [abstract concept].

Contextualize your message in relation to the commentator's evaluations regarding the issue of your racial history.

Contextualize your message in relation to the commentator's evaluations regarding the issue of your racial history by citing unspecific instances of appealing to those of a differing racial history.

Contextualize your message in relation to the commentator's evaluations regarding the issue of your racial history by citing a specific instance of appealing to those of a differing racial history, as well as to those who share your personal racial history.

Contextualize your message in relation to the commentator's evaluations regarding the issue of your racial history by citing a specific instance of appealing to those of a differing racial history, while highlighting the presence of an icon symbolic of the history of [unanimously hated act of racial subjugation].

Contextualize your racial identity as it pertains to your current status as a candidate for [relevant office].

Contextualize your racial identity in relation to the commentator's evaluations that yours is an extreme example of that identity.

Contextualize your racial identity in relation to the commentator's evaluations that yours is an example of that identity that is not extreme enough.

Contextualize your racial identity in relation to a specific example of your racial identity having a negative impact in a particular political region.

Contextualize your racial identity in relation to media analysis done in order to gauge its effect on your status as a candidate for [relevant office] among various different ethnic communities.

Now, take a moment from contextualizing your person in order to highlight the fact that only within the last approximately fourteen days has the issue of [relevant ethnic origin] become problematic as it pertains to your status as candidate for [relevant office] of [relevant nation].

Take a moment from contextualizing your person in order to highlight the commentator's evaluations that your status as candidate for [relevant office] is merely an example of [relevant policy initiative].

Take a moment from contextualizing your person in order to highlight the commentator's evaluations that your status as candidate for [relevant office] is merely a reaction to [unanimously hated act of racial subjugation] by [relevant political ideology].

Take a moment from contextualizing your person in order to address the opinions of a specific figure from your life as a private citizen.

Take a moment from contextualizing your person in order to address the negative effects that the opinions of this specific figure from your life as a private citizen could have on racial issues.

Take a moment from contextualizing your person in order to address the negative effects that the opinions of this specific figure from your life as a private citizen could have on [list of abstract concepts] regarding [relevant nation].

Take a moment from contextualizing your person in order to address the negative effects that the opinions of this specific figure from your life as a private citizen could have on the sensibilities of [relevant dichotomy].

[Pause for applause]

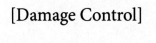

[Damage Control]

- You must distance yourself from said person.

- You must distance your message from said person.

- You must re-condemn in unequivocal terms the statements of said person.

• You must acknowledge that for some, questions nag of said person:

1) Did you know the fierce criticism of domestic and foreign policy of said person?

(Well of course you did of said person.)

2) Did you hear controversial church statements from said person?

(Well of course you did from said person.)

3) Did you disagree with various political views of said person?

(Well of course you did of said person.)

4) Did your audience have moments when they disagreed with views of their equivalent said person?

(Well of course you hope of their person.)

• You must create some gulf between the statements of said person and the historic lineage of contentious statements made by equally opinionated commentators.

> • You must differentiate between the statements of said person and the historic lineage of faith-based social commentary.

On both points you must counter:

1) Statements of said person are of a profoundly distorted country.

2) Statements of said person are reverse-racism.

3A) Statements of said person are critical of [list of positive qualities] Zionism.

3B) Statements of said person are uncritical of [list of negative qualities] Islamic extremism.

• You must acknowledge partial-audience's inability to suspend disbelief regarding your personal statements on said person's statements.

Base this acknowledgement on:

1) Your personal history.

2) Your personal ideology.

3A) Your personal sense of worth.

3B) Your personal conception of something in its perfection.

- You must ask some rhetorical questions:

    1) Why ever knowingly know said person?

    2) Why ever knowingly religiously congregate with said person?

• You must acknowledge that you yourself would condemn said person had your relations with said person been limited to:

1) The footage of said person perpetually aired on non-specific television networks.

2) The footage of said person perpetually streamed on a specific user-generated video-sharing website.

• You must acknowledge that you would condemn said religious institution had your relations with said religious institution been limited to the hyperbolic and oversimplified portraits presented by various pundits.

• You must now reconstruct the image of said person by highlighting overlooked biographical information of said person by:

1) Presenting yourself as a reliable character witness regarding said person.

2) Providing the general date in which you first met said person.

3) Attesting to said person's influence on your religious affiliation.

4A) Attesting to said person's influence on broad aspects of your personal moral convictions.

4B) Attesting to said person's influence on specific aspects of your personal moral convictions.

- You must now reconstruct the image of said person by presenting the following biographical facts that will appeal to said person's character:

1) Present the fact that said person possesses a history of military service.

2) Present the fact that said person has been affiliated with prestigious institutions.

3A) Present the fact that said person has been involved in various faith-based initiatives for an approximate amount of time.

3B) Present specific examples of various faith-based initiatives undertaken by said person.

• You must present your first memory of the religious institution in which you first became acquainted with said person by using an excerpt from your own memoir:

quote plural noun past particle verb preposition verb comma preposition verb preposition possessive passive pronoun plural noun conjunction verb adjective comma indefinite article adjective noun active verb definite article possessive noun noun preposition preposition definite article plural noun period ellipsis conjunction preposition adjective adjective noun hyphen abstract noun exclamation point hyphen personal pronoun verb pronoun adjective semicolon preposition definite article noun preposition pronoun noun comma preposition definite article plural noun preposition plural noun preposition definite article noun comma personal pronoun passive verb definite article plural noun preposition adjective adjective plural noun continuous verb preposition definite article plural noun preposition proper noun conjunction proper noun comma proper noun conjunction proper noun comma definite article plural noun preposition definite article possessive noun noun comma possessive proper noun noun preposition adjective plural noun period plural adjective plural noun hyphen preposition noun comma conjunction abstract noun comma conjunction abstract noun hyphen simple past verb pronoun noun comma possessive pronoun noun semicolon definite article noun pronoun auxiliary verb passive verb passive verb pronoun noun comma definite article plural noun pronoun plural noun semicolon preposition pronoun adjective noun comma preposition pronoun adjective noun comma passive verb adverb adverb indefinite article noun continuous verb definite article noun preposition indefinite article plural noun preposition adjective plural noun conjunction preposition indefinite article comparative adjective noun period pronoun plural noun conjunction plural noun passive verb preposition adverb adjective conjunction adjective comma adjective conjunction noun conjunction adjective semicolon preposition continuous verb pronoun noun comma definite article plural noun conjunction plural noun passive verb pronoun indefinite article noun preposition verb plural noun conjunction plural pronoun negative contraction verb adverb verb noun adjective ellipsis plural noun conjunction adjective plural noun auxiliary verb verb conjunction verb hyphen conjunction preposition pronoun plural pronoun auxiliary verb verb adverb verb period endquote

• You must highlight that the above excerpt is an accurate portrayal of the religious institution in which you first became acquainted with said person.

• You must compare the religious institution in which you first became acquainted with said person to other religious institutions that cater to a similar racial demographic.

• You must state that religious institutions that cater to a similar racial demographic as the religious institution in which you first became acquainted with said person do much to encapsulate the many facets of that particular racial demographic.

• You must set up some dichotomies that act as examples of the aforementioned statement:

> definite article [doctor] conjunction definite article [welfare mom] comma definite article [model student] conjunction definite article [former gangbanger] period

• You must state that religious institutions that cater to a similar racial demographic as the religious institution in which you first became acquainted with said person share a list of similar attributes and occurrences.

•You must provide some examples and dichotomies for ↑bove statement:

possessive proper noun plural noun verb adjective preposition [raucous laughter] conjunction adverb [bawdy humour] period plural pronoun present indicative plural verb adjective preposition [dancing] comma [screaming] conjunction [shouting] adverb auxiliary verb [seem jarring] preposition definite article [untrained ear] period definite article noun continuous verb idiom definite article [kindness] conjunction [cruelty] comma definite article [fierce intelligence] conjunction definite article [shocking ignorance] comma definite article [struggles] conjunction [successes] comma definite article [love] conjunction adverb comma definite article [bitterness] conjunction [bias] adverb verb phrase definite article [particular race experience] preposition [relevant nation] period

• You must suggest that above examples rationalize your association with said person.

        • You must acknowledge that there are obvious flaws associated with said person.

• You must counter above acknowledgment by presenting a list of biographical notes that further rationalize your association with said person:

1) Your relationship with said person has progressed to the point of familial non-judgment.

2) Your relationship with said person has progressed your spiritual impulses.

3) Said person presided over [relevant civil ritual] of your spouse.

4) Said person presided over [relevant religious ritual] of your children.

5A) Said person has never in your presence made any comment that could be interpreted as pejorative toward any particular racial demographic.

5B) Said person has never in your presence acted in a way that could be interpreted as disrespectful towards [specific racial demographic].

• You must suggest that said person's flaws run parallel to the flaws of [personal racial demographic] and highlight his history of personal service towards [personal racial demographic].

• You must suggest that you must forgive said person's flaws just as you must forgive the flaws of [personal racial demographic].

• You must suggest that you must forgive said person's flaws just as you must forgive the flaws of [relevant matriarchal figure].

- You must highlight the fact that [relevant matriarchal figure]:

  1) Had a significant and essential role in your personal development.

  2) Always put your interests ahead of her self-interest.

  3) [General statement expressing said matriarchal figure's deep emotional endearment towards you]

  4) Has in your presence made comments that could be interpreted as pejorative toward [specific racial demographic], despite the fact that you are yourself a member of [specific racial demographic].

- You must connect all aforementioned people to your personal narrative.

- You must connect all aforementioned people to the narrative of [relevant nation].

- You must express your [relevant abstract concept] for [relevant nation].

[Pause for applause]

[Understanding This Noun]

plural pronoun   [will see this as]

indefinite article

noun   adverb

[justify or

excuse comments]

pronoun   second person singular verb

[simply inexcusable]   **period**

personal pronoun

[can assure you

it is not]   **period**

personal pronoun   verb

[the politically safe]   noun

simple past tense verb

verb   preposition

[move on from]   adjective   noun

conjunction   adverb

[hope that it fades into

the woodwork]   **period**

plural pronoun   auxiliary verb

[dismiss said person]

adverb   indefinite article

[crank]

conjunction   indefinite article

[demagogue]   comma

adverb   conjunction   pronoun

[have dismissed specific

supporter of opponent]

comma   preposition

definite article

[aftermath of   pronoun

recent statements]

comma   adverb   present verb

[some deep-seated racial bias] **period**

conjunction

[race is
an issue]

                        conjunction

personal pronoun

               verb

adjective

[nation cannot afford]

preposition

[ignore right now]

period

pronoun

simple past tense verb

         auxiliary verb

present verb

       definite article

[same mistake that
said person]

       simple past tense verb

preposition

pronoun

[offending sermons about
relevant nation]

       hyphen

preposition

[simplify]

conjunction

[stereotype]

conjunction

[amplify the negative]

preposition

definite article   noun

conjunction

       pronoun

[distorts reality]

period

[the fact is]
conjunction   definite article
[comments that have been made]
conjunction   definite article
[issues that have surfaced]
preposition   definite article   adjective
adjective   plural noun
[reflect the complexities of]
noun   preposition
adjective   noun
pronoun   contraction
[never really worked through]
hyphen   indefinite article   noun
[of our union]
conjunction
plural pronoun
[have yet to perfect]

period

conjunction
conjunction   plural pronoun
[walk away]   noun
comma
conjunction   plural pronoun
[simply retreat]
preposition   pronoun
[respective corners]
comma
plural pronoun
auxiliary verb   adverb
auxiliary verb   adjective
preposition
[come together and solve]
plural noun   preposition
[healthcare]   comma

51

[education]   comma
definite article   noun
[to find good jobs]
                                preposition
[every citizen of relevant nation]   period

[understanding   **[pause for applause]**
          understanding this reality
                    requires a reminder]
          preposition   conjunction
                    plural pronoun   verb
          preposition   adjective   noun
                                                period

          adverb   [specific author]   adverb
                    verb   comma
quote
          [the past isn't dead and buried]

          period

          [in fact comma it isn't even past]

                                        period
                                        endquote

                    plural pronoun
[do not need to recite here
                    the history]
          preposition   adjective   noun
                    preposition   adjective   noun
                                                period

          conjunction   plural pronoun   verb
                    [need to remind
                    ourselves that]
adverb   adjective

[of the disparities
that exist]
preposition   definite article
adjective   noun   adverb   auxiliary verb
verb   [directly traced to
inequalities passed]
adverb   preposition
[an earlier generation]
conjunction   passive verb
[under the brutal legacy of   [unanimously
hated act of
racial subjugation]   conjunction
specific
discriminatory
legislation]
period

[segregated schools]
superlative singular verb
comma
conjunction
present second singular verb
comma
[inferior schools]
semicolon
plural pronoun
adverb
verb contraction
adjective
adverb
comma
noun
plural noun
adverb
[specific historical court case]

[pause for applause]

comma

conjunction

definite article

[inferior education]

adverb

verb

comma

adverb

conjunction

adverb

comma

present verb

verb

definite article

[pervasive achievement gap]

preposition

possessive noun

[specific racial backgrounds

used as dichotomy

students]

period

[legalized discrimination]   hyphen

adverb   plural noun

verb   passive verb

comma

[often through violence]

comma   preposition

progressive verb   noun

comma

conjunction   plural noun

verb   adverb

passive verb   adverb

[country of origin] hyphen

[country of origin business owners]

comma   conjunction

[specific race homeowners]
   passive verb   adverb   noun
[specific government
agency mortgages]   comma   conjunction
   plural noun verb   passive verb
[from unions]   comma
    conjunction   definite article
[police force]   comma
    conjunction
[fire departments]   hyphen passive verb
     [that specific race
        families
    could not
     amass any meaningful] noun
    [to bequeath to
       future generations]
  period

pronoun
    noun [helps explain
       the wealth
    and income gap
      between]
  adjective   conjunction
   adjective   comma
 conjunction   definite article
   [concentrated pockets
     of poverty]
    pronoun   plural verb
preposition   conjunction
 adjective preposition [today's urban and
     rural communities]

period

   indefinite article
    [lack of economic opportunity

55

among]

adjective   plural noun
                    comma
          conjunction   definite article
[shame]
                    conjunction
     [frustration]
               pronoun   passive verb
     preposition   adverb
                    conjunction   adjective
                    preposition
[provide for one's family]   comma
          passive verb   preposition
                    definite article
     [erosion of specific race families]   hyphen
          indefinite article   noun
                    [that welfare policies
     preposition
               adjective   plural noun
                    auxiliary verb
          have worsened]   **period**

          conjunction   definite article
          [lack of basic services]
                    preposition   adverb
               adjective
                    [urban specific
                         race neighbourhoods]
                                        hyphen
          [parks for kids to play in]   comma
          [police walking the beat]   comma
          [regular garbage pickup]   conjunction
     [building code enforcement]   hyphen
                    pronoun   passive verb
               verb   indefinite article
[cycle of violence]   comma
          [blight and neglect]   adverb   verb

56

[to haunt us]
period

pronoun   [is the reality]
preposition
pronoun   [said person]
conjunction   adjective
proper noun   hyphen
plural proper noun   [of his generation]
verb   preposition
period

plural pronoun
simple past tense verb
preposition   noun   preposition
definite article
[late fifties]
conjunction
[early sixties]   **comma**
indefinite article   noun
conjunction   [segregation]
verb   adverb   definite article
[law of the land]
conjunction [opportunity]   verb
[systematically constricted]   **period**

contraction   adjective
third person singular present verb
adverb conjunction
adjective   verb   preposition
[the face of discrimination]   **comma**
conjunction   adverb
conjunction   adjective
gendered plural noun
conjunction   gendered plural noun
[overcame the odds]
semicolon   conjunction

adjective   verb
   adjective   preposition   verb
[a way out of no way]   preposition
          plural pronoun   adjective
   objective pronoun   [who came after them]
period

   idiom   adjective   pronoun   pronoun   [scratched and clawed]
pronoun noun   preposition   verb indefinite article   noun
   preposition   [the nation-specific dream] comma   adverb
passive verb   pronoun [who didn't make it]   hyphen   adjective
   pronoun subjunctive verb   [ultimately defeated] comma
     preposition   adjective   noun   conjunction
      pronoun   comma [by discrimination] **period**

pronoun   [legacy of defeat] verb   verb phrase   preposition
   [future generations]   hyphen   adjective   [young men]
    conjunction   [increasingly young women] pronoun
   possessive plural pronoun   verb [standing on street corners]
conjunction [languishing in our prisons] comma preposition abstract noun
 conjunction plural noun preposition definite article   noun   **period**

adverb preposition adjective plural proper noun pronoun simple past verb
  verb noun comma [questions of race] comma   conjunction noun
comma [continue to define] **pronoun** [worldview in fundamental ways]
     period

   preposition   definite article   gendered plural noun
     conjunction   gendered plural noun   preposition
   [said person's generation]   comma   definite article
[memories of humiliation] conjunction [doubt]   conjunction   [fear]
 auxiliary verb adverb verb adverb semicolon   conjunction
  singular present indicative verb   definite article [anger] conjunction
    definite article   [bitterness of those years]   **period**

     adjective noun [may not get expressed in public]   comma
idiom [specific race co-workers] conjunction adjective plural noun

period

conjunction   pronoun   auxiliary verb   [find voice in the barbershop]
conjunction   [around the kitchen table]   **period**

    preposition   plural noun   comma adjective   noun
    verb   [exploited by politicians]   comma   preposition
        [gin up votes]   preposition   adjective   plural noun
comma   conjunction   preposition   verb phrase
        [for a politician's own failings]   **period**

conjunction   [occasionally it finds voice]
        preposition   definite article   noun
preposition   [day of the week]   noun   comma
        [in the pulpit and in the pews]   **period**

definite article   noun   pronoun   ·   adverb
        adjective   plural noun   verb
            [surprised to hear that anger]   preposition
    adjective   preposition   [said person's sermons]
            adverb   verb   plural pronoun
[of the old truism]
            conjunction   definite article
            [most segregated hour in
                                    specific nationality]
noun   [occurs on Sunday morning] **period**

[pause for applause]

    adjective   noun   [is not always productive]
        semicolon   adverb   comma   adjective
[too often it distracts]   noun   preposition
            [solving real problems]   semicolon   pronoun
    verb   plural pronoun   preposition   adjective
        verb   plural pronoun   adjective
[complicity in our condition]   comma
                    conjunction   present verb

59

indefinite article   proper noun   hyphen
proper noun   noun   [from forging the alliances]
pronoun   verb   [to]   verb [about real change] **period**

conjunction   [the anger is real]   semicolon
[it is powerful]   semicolon
conjunction   preposition   verb
verb   pronoun   adverb   comma
[to condemn it without understanding]
pronoun   plural noun   comma   adverb
[serves to widen the chasm of misunderstanding] adverb
verb   preposition   definite article   plural noun   **period**

preposition noun   comma   [a similar anger exists]
preposition plural noun   [of the specific race community]   **period**

adjective   ˇ[working- and middle-class specific race]
plural proper noun   [don't feel that]   plural pronoun
verb   past particle verb   adverb [privileged by their race]   **period**

possessive pronoun   noun   [is the immigrant experience]
hyphen idiom   contraction   verb   comma
[no one's handed]   plural pronoun   noun   comma
contraction [built it from scratch] **period**

contraction   [worked hard all their lives]
comma   adjective plural noun   conjunction
preposition   verb   [their jobs shipped overseas]
conjunction   plural pronoun   [pension dumped]
preposition indefinite article   noun preposition noun **period**

[they are anxious about]   plural pronoun   plural noun
comma   conjunction   [feel their dreams slipping] adverb
semicolon   preposition   [an era of stagnant wages]
conjunction   [global competition]
comma   noun   verb   preposition   auxiliary verb
past particle   verb [as a zero-sum game] comma   preposition

pronoun   pronoun   [dreams come at my expense]   **period**

conjunction   adverb   plural pronoun   [are told to]
    verb   plural pronoun   plural noun   [to a school across town]
      semicolon   adverb   plural pronoun
  verb   conjunction   indefinite article   proper noun   auxiliary verb
verb   indefinite article   noun   [in landing a good job]
    conjunction   indefinite article   noun
  [in a good college because]   preposition   indefinite article
    noun   [that they themselves
            never committed]   semicolon   conjunction
contraction   verb   pronoun   plural pronoun   plural noun
[about crime in urban neighbourhoods]   auxiliary verb
      adverb   [prejudiced]   comma   [resentment builds]
    preposition   noun   **period**

[like the anger]
       preposition   definite article
  adjective   noun comma
       adjective   plural noun
         [aren't always expressed in
           polite company]   **period**

    conjunction   plural pronoun
      auxiliary verb   [helped shape the
          political landscape]   preposition
[at least a generation]   **period**

      [anger over welfare]
          conjunction
    [affirmative action]   verb
[forge the
    specific political figure
        coalition]   **period**

   plural noun   adverb
         [exploited fears of crime]

preposition

plural pronoun

[own electoral ends]   **period**

[talk-show hosts]   conjunction

[conservative commentators]   verb

[entire careers unmasking]

adjective   plural noun

preposition   noun

conjunction   [dismissing legitimate discussions

of racial injustice]

conjunction

[inequality as

mere political correctness]

conjunction

adjective   noun

period

[pause for applause]

adverb   conjunction

adjective   noun

[often proved counterproductive]

comma   conjunction

verb   plural pronoun

adjective   plural noun

[distracted attention]   preposition

definite article   [real culprits]

preposition   definite article

[middle-class squeeze]

hyphen   indefinite article

adjective   noun

[rife with inside dealing]   comma

[questionable accounting practices]

comma   conjunction

[short-term greed]

semicolon   indefinite article

[name of specific capitol city]
[dominated by lobbyists]   conjunction
[special interests]   semicolon
          adjective   plural noun   conjunction
[favour the few over the many]   **period**

conjunction   conjunction
          comma   adverb   [wish away the resentments of]
adjective   plural proper noun
               comma   adverb
verb   plural pronoun
          conjunction   [misguided or
                    even racist] comma   preposition
     verb   plural pronoun
               verb   adjective
[in legitimate concerns]
                    hyphen   pronoun   adverb
     verb   definite article
               adjective   noun
     comma   conjunction
[blocks the path to]   noun   **period**

pronoun
               [is where we are
                    right now]
          period

          contraction   indefinite article
adjective   noun
                    [we've been stuck in
                    for years]   **period**

[contrary to the claims of]
                              adjective
                                   preposition
     personal pronoun   plural noun
                                   comma

63

adjective   conjunction   adjective

comma

personal pronoun   verb

[never been so naïve

as to believe]

conjunction

collective plural pronoun

auxiliary verb

verb   preposition

collective plural pronoun

adjective   plural noun

[in a single election cycle]

comma

conjunction

[with a single candidacy]

hyphen

adverb

[pause for applause]

comma

adverb   indefinite article

noun

[as imperfect as my own]

period

conjunction

[I have asserted a]

adjective

noun

hyphen

[a conviction rooted in]

personal possessive pronoun

noun

[in God]

conjunction

personal possessive pronoun

noun

64

[in the people of
relevant nation]

hyphen

adverb

verb

[together
we can move beyond]

adjective

preposition

collective pronoun

adjective

adjective

plural noun

comma

conjunction

conjunction

[in fact we have no
choice if]

plural pronoun

indicative plural verb

preposition

verb   adverb

[the path of
a more perfect]

noun

period

preposition   definite article   adjective
noun   comma   adjective
noun   [means embracing the burdens of]   collective plural pronoun
noun   [without becoming victims of]   collective plural pronoun
noun   **period**

pronoun   [means continuing to insist on]   indefinite article
[full measure of]   noun   [in every aspect of]   adjective noun
period

conjunction   pronoun
          adverb   [means binding our particular]   plural noun
hyphen   [for better]   noun
      comma   [and better]   plural noun
              comma   [and better]   plural verb
hyphen
          adverb   [the larger aspirations of] adjective plural proper noun
                  em dash   definite article   adjective
gendered noun   [struggling to break the glass ceiling]
                  comma   definite article   adjective
gendered noun   [whose been laid off]
comma   definite article   [immigrant trying to feed his family]
                  period

          conjunction   pronoun
[means taking full responsibility for]   collective plural pronoun
                  adjective   plural noun   hyphen
          preposition   [demanding more from our] plural noun
              comma   conjunction
                  [spending more time with our]   plural noun
comma   conjunction   [reading to]   plural pronoun
      comma   conjunction   [teaching]   plural pronoun
          [that while they may face]   plural noun
conjunction   noun   preposition
pronoun   adjective   plural noun   comma
      pronoun   [must never succumb to]
noun   conjunction   noun   semicolon
          plural pronoun   [must always believe]
                  [pause for applause]
          plural pronoun   [must always believe]   adverb
      [they can write their own]   noun   **period**

              [ironically]
                  comma
                          pronoun
      [quintessentially]
                  adjective

                  66

em dash

[and yes]

comma

[conservative]

hyphen

noun

[of self-help
found frequent]

noun

preposition

[said person's sermons]

period

conjunction

adverb

personal pronoun

adjective

noun

[too often failed to]

verb   verb

[that embarking

on a program of]

noun

adverb

verb

[a belief that society can]

verb

period

[the profound mistake of]

[said person's] plural noun   verb   pronoun   adjective

gendered pronoun   [spoke about racism in our]   noun   period

contraction   conjunction   gendered pronoun   verb

preposition   [if our society was static]   semicolon

preposition   [if no progress has been made]   semicolon

preposition   [if this country]

hyphen   indefinite article
noun   [that has made it possible for]
adjective   preposition   possessive gendered pronoun
adjective   plural noun   [to run for the highest office]
preposition   definite article   noun   conjunction
[build a coalition of]
[white]   conjunction   [black]   semicolon
[latino]   conjunction   [asian]   comma
[rich]   conjunction   [poor]   comma
[young]   conjunction   [old]   em dash
verb   [still irrevocably bound to]   indefinite article
adjective   noun period

[pause for applause]

conjunction   pronoun   [we know]
em dash   pronoun   [we have seen]
hyphen verb [that
specific nation
can change]   **period**

pronoun   [is the true genius of]   pronoun
noun   **period**

pronoun   [we have already achieved]   verb
collective plural pronoun
noun   hyphen
[the audacity to]   noun
hyphen   preposition   pronoun
[we can and must achieve]   noun
period

preposition   definite article
adjective   noun   comma
[the path to a more perfect]   noun
verb   [acknowledging that what ails the]   **adjective**   noun
[does not just exist in the minds of]   **adjective**   plural noun

semicolon   [that the legacy of]   noun
hyphen   [and current incidents of]   noun
         comma   conjunction   adjective
     adjective   conjunction   preposition
       definite article   noun   hyphen
[are real]   conjunction
       [must be addressed]   **period**

     adverb   adverb
       [with words]   comma   preposition
           [with deeds]   hyphen   preposition
   [investing in our]   plural noun
       [and our]   plural noun
semicolon   [by enforcing our]   adjective   plural noun
[and ensuring]   noun   [in our]   adjective   noun
semicolon   [by providing this]   noun
     [with ladders of]   noun
[that were unavailable for previous]   plural noun   **period**

pronoun   [requires all]   plural proper noun
      adverb   verb   [that your dreams do not]   auxiliary verb
adverb   verb   [at the expense of my dreams]   semicolon
     [that investing in]   definite article
          [health]   comma
            [welfare]   comma
        conjunction   [education]
   conjunction   [black]
conjunction   [brown]
   conjunction   [white]   plural noun
     [will ultimately help all of]   proper noun
   verb   **period**

[pause for applause]

    [in the end]
       comma   adverb
     comma   pronoun

verb
    verb   preposition
verb
[nothing more]   comma   conjunction
      [nothing less]   comma   conjunction
      pronoun
         [all the world's
            great religions]
                  verb
hyphen
      [that we do unto others as we
             would have them do unto us]
                  period

verb
    collective plural pronoun
           [be our brother's keeper]
                  comma
noun [tells us]   **period**

verb
    collective plural pronoun
           [be our sister's keeper] **period**

verb
    collective plural pronoun
           verb pronoun
[common stake
       we all have]   preposition   adjective   pronoun
                comma
                conjunction
[let our politics reflect]   adjective   noun   idiom
            period

preposition   [we have a choice in this]   noun   **period**

   [we can accept a politics that breeds]

noun   comma   conjunction
noun   comma   conjunction
noun   **period**

[we can tackle race
        only as]   noun   hyphen
                    [as we did in the
                            specific former athlete
                                        trial]   **hyphen**
            [or in the wake of]   noun
comma   [as we did in the aftermath of
                    specific natural disaster]   **hyphen**
        conjunction   adverb
            [fodder for the nightly]   noun   **period**

[we can play
            said person's sermons
                        on] adjective noun
        comma   adjective   noun conjunction
        [talk about them from now until the]   noun
                        comma   conjunction
[make the only question in this]   noun
                [whether or not the]   proper pronoun   noun
verb   [that I somehow believe or
    sympathize with his] adjective   adjective   plural noun   **period**

[we can pounce on some gaffe by]   indefinite article
[supporter of current opponent]   adverb   noun
                [that she's playing the]   adjective   noun
comma   conjunction
        [we can speculate on whether]   adjective   gendered noun
            [will all flock to
                name of future opponent
                        in the] adjective   noun
[regardless of his]   plural pronoun **period**

71

possessive
        plural
            pronoun

[can
        do
            that]

period

[but if we]
verb
comma
personal pronoun
[can tell you that
in the next]
noun
comma
[we'll be talking about
some other]
noun
period

conjunction
adverb
[another one]
period

conjunction
[then another one]
period

[and nothing will change]
period

pronoun
[is one option]
period

[or]   comma   [at this]   noun   comma
[in this]   noun   comma
collective plural pronoun
[can come together and]   verb   comma
quote
[not this time]   **period**
endquote

[this time we want to talk]
preposition   definite article   adjective   plural noun
[that are stealing the future of]
    adjective   [children]   conjunction
      adjective   [children]   conjunction
    adjective   [children]   conjunction
      adjective   [children]   conjunction
    adjective   [children]   **period**

[this time we want to reject]
definite article   noun   adverb   verb   collective plural pronoun
[that these kids can't learn]
    semicolon   [that those kids who don't]
verb preposition   collective plural pronoun
    [are somebody else's problem]   **period**

definite article   [children of]
    [specific nation]
    [are not those kids]   comma
[they are our]   plural pronoun   comma
    conjunction   [we will not let them]   verb
preposition   preposition   indefinite article
    [twenty-first century]   noun   **period**

[not this]   noun   **period**

[this time we want
    to talk about]
    conjunction
    definite article
[lines in the]
    adjective noun
    [are filled]
    preposition
    plural noun
    conjunction
plural noun

conjunction

plural noun

[who do not have]

adjective   noun

semicolon

[who don't have the]

noun

[on their own]

[to overcome the]

adjective   plural noun

[in specific capitol city]

comma

conjunction

[who can take them on if]

collective plural noun

[do it together]

period

adjective   noun

collective plural pronoun   [want to talk about]

definite article

[shuttered mills]

adverb

[once provided a decent life]

preposition

gendered plural noun

conjunction

gendered plural noun

[of every race]

comma

conjunction

[the homes for sale]

adverb

[once belonged]

preposition

plural proper noun [from every religion]

comma

[every region]

comma

[every walk of life]   **period**

adjective   noun
collective plural pronoun   [want to talk about]   definite article
[fact that]

definite article
[real problem is not]   conjunction
[someone who doesn't
look like]   pronoun

auxiliary verb
[take your job]

semicolon

contraction   conjunction
definite article   [corporation you work for will]   verb
pronoun

plural pronoun
preposition
[nothing more than a profit]
period

[pause for applause]

adjective noun
collective plural pronoun   [want to talk about]
definite article
gendered plural noun   conjunction
gendered plural noun   preposition
[every colour and creed]
pronoun
[serve together]   comma
conjunction
[fight together]   comma
conjunction
[bleed together]   preposition
[the same proud flag]   **period**

76

collective plural pronoun

verb   preposition

verb   preposition

[how to bring them home]

preposition

[a war]

conjunction

[never should've been authorized]

conjunction

[never should've been waged] . **comma**

[pause for applause]

conjunction

collective plural pronoun

verb   preposition

verb   preposition

[how we'll show]

collective plural pronoun

noun

[by caring for them]   **comma**

conjunction

[their families] **comma**

conjunction

verb

plural pronoun

[the benefits they have earned]   **period**

[pause for applause]

personal pronoun

[would not be running for

relevant office]

conjunction

personal pronoun

[didn't believe with all my] **noun**

pronoun

pronoun

    verb

      pronoun

[the vast majority of]   plural proper noun

    [want for this country]   **period**

    adjective

        noun   [may never be perfect]

          comma   conjunction

          [generation after generation]

                auxiliary verb

verb

    [that it can]   adverb

        [be perfected] **period**

    conjunction   noun

            comma

    [whenever I find myself feeling]   noun

  conjunction

      noun   [about this possibility]

comma

   [what gives me the most]   noun

      [is the next generation]

  hyphen   definite article

      [young people]

          pronoun

[attitudes] conjunction

  [beliefs]   conjunction

    [openness]   preposition

        noun

[have already made history in this] noun   **period**

[pause for applause]

[Close with an Anecdote]

i. relevance to topic

you have reached the end of your speech

and you will finish your speech with an anecdote

this anecdote that you will end your speech with

is particularly relevant to the topic of the speech

you are now finishing

this anecdote that you will end your speech with

is an anecdote that you have performed at least once before

and is particularly relevant to the topic of the speech

you are now finishing

this anecdote that you will end your speech with

is an anecdote that you have performed at least once before

on the birthday of a figure particularly relevant

to the topic of the speech you are

now finishing

this anecdote that you will end your speech with

is an anecdote that you have performed at least once before

at a particularly relevant location

on the birthday of a figure particularly relevant

to the topic of the speech

you are now

finishing

this anecdote that you will end your speech with

contains a person of a specific name

who works on your campaign for a specific office

this anecdote that you will end your speech with

contains a person of a specific name

and of a specific gender

who works on your campaign for a specific office

this anecdote that you will end your speech with

contains a person of a specific name

and of a specific gender

and of a specific age

who works on your campaign for a specific office

this anecdote that you will end your speech with

contains a person of a specific name

and of a specific gender

and of a specific age

and of a specific race

who works on your campaign for a specific office

this anecdote that you will end your speech with

contains a person of a specific name

and of a specific gender

and of a specific age

and of a specific race

who works on your campaign for a specific office

in a specific capacity

this anecdote that you will end your speech with

contains a person of a specific name

and of a specific gender

and of a specific age

and of a specific race

who works on your campaign for a specific office

in a specific capacity

in a specific city

this anecdote that you will end your speech with

contains a person of a specific name

and of a specific gender

and of a specific age

and of a specific race

who works on your campaign for a specific office

in a specific capacity

in a specific city

and primarily with a specific racial community

this anecdote that you will end your speech with

contains a person of a specific name

and of a specific gender

and of a specific age

and of a specific race

who works on your campaign for a specific office

in a specific capacity

in a specific city

and primarily with a specific racial community

for a specific amount of time

this anecdote that you will end your speech with

contains a person of a specific name

and of a specific gender

and of a specific age

and of a specific race

who works on your campaign for a specific office

in a specific capacity

in a specific city

and primarily with a specific racial community

for a specific amount of time

who was asked why they were working on

your campaign specifically

this anecdote that you will end your speech with

contains a person of a specific name

and of a specific gender

and of a specific age

and of a specific race

who works on your campaign for a specific office

in a specific capacity

in a specific city

and primarily with a specific racial community

for a specific amount of time

who was asked why they were working on

your campaign specifically

among a group of other supporters of your campaign

for a specific office

this anecdote that you will end your speech with contains

another anecdote

this anecdote that you will end your speech with contains

another anecdote

told by the person of a specific name

contained in the framing anecdote

this anecdote that you will end your speech with contains

another anecdote

told by the person of a specific name

contained in the framing anecdote

and concerns the person of a specific name's mother

this anecdote that you will end your speech with contains

another anecdote

told by the person of a specific name

contained in the framing anecdote

and concerns the person of a specific name's mother

and the tumour that was developing in the person

of a specific name's mother's body

this anecdote that you will end your speech with contains

another anecdote

told by the person of a specific name

contained in the framing anecdote

and concerns the person of a specific name's mother

and the days of work that the person

of a specific name's mother had to miss

because of the tumour that was developing

in the person of a specific name's

mother's body

this anecdote that you will end your speech with contains

another anecdote told by the person of a specific name

contained in the framing anecdote

and concerns the person of a specific name's mother

and the job that the person of a specific name's

mother lost

because of the days of work that the person of a specific name's

mother had to miss

because of the tumour that was developing in the person of a specific

name's mother's body

this anecdote that you will end your speech with contains

another anecdote told by the person of a specific name

contained in the framing anecdote

and concerns the person of a specific name's mother

and the health coverage that the person of a specific name's

mother lost

because of the job that the person of a specific name's mother lost

because of the days of work that the person of a specific name's

mother had to miss

because of the tumour that was developing in the

person of a specific name's

mother's body

this anecdote that you will end your speech with contains

another anecdote told by the person of a specific name

contained in the framing anecdote

and concerns the person of a specific name's mother

and the bankruptcy that the person of a specific name's mother

had to file for

because of health coverage that the person of a specific

name's mother lost

because of the job that the person of a specific name's mother lost

because of the days of work that the person of a specific name's

mother had to miss

because of the tumour that was developing in the person of a specific

name's mother's body

this anecdote that you will end your speech with contains

another anecdote told by the person of a specific name

contained in the framing anecdote

and concerns the person of a specific name's mother

and the decisions that the person of a specific name had to make

because of the bankruptcy the person of a specific name's mother

had to file for

because of health coverage that the person of a specific name's

mother lost

because of the job that the person of a specific name's

mother lost

because of the days of work that the person of a specific name's

mother had to miss

because of the tumour that was developing in the person of a specific

name's mother's body

this anecdote that you will end your speech with contains

another anecdote told by the person of a specific name

contained in the framing anecdote

and concerns the person of a specific name's mother

and their economic situation

this anecdote that you will end your speech with contains

another anecdote told by the person of a specific name

this anecdote that you will end your speech with contains

contained in the framing anecdote

another anecdote told by the person of a specific name

this anecdote that you will end your speech with contains

and concerns the person of a specific name's mother

contained in the framing anecdote

another anecdote told by the person of a specific name

this anecdote that you will end your speech with contains

and their economic situation

and concerns the person of a specific name's mother

contained in the framing anecdote

another anecdote told by the person of a specific name

this anecdote that you will end your speech with contains

as it specifically pertains to the cost of food

and the decisions that the person of a specific name had to make

and concerns the person of a specific name's mother

contained in the framing anecdote

another anecdote told by the person of a specific name

because of their economic situation

and the decisions that the person of a specific name

had to make

and concerns the person of a specific name's mother

contained in the framing anecdote

as it specifically pertains to the cost of food

concerning mustard and relish sandwiches

and the decisions that the person of a specific name

had to make

and concerns the person of a specific name's mother

because of their economic situation

concerning the affordability of mustard and relish sandwiches

and the decisions that the person of a specific name had to make

as it specifically pertains to the cost of food

when compared to other forms of nutrition

at a specific age

because of their economic situation

concerning the affordability of mustard and

relish sandwiches

as it specifically pertains to the cost of food

when compared to other forms of nutrition

because of their economic situation

as it specifically pertains to the cost of food

this anecdote that you will end your speech with contains

another anecdote told by the person of a specific name

this anecdote that you will end your speech with contains

contained in the framing anecdote

another anecdote told by the person of a specific name

and concerns the person of a specific name's mother

contained in the framing anecdote

and the decisions that the person of a specific name had to make

and concerns the person of a specific name's mother

at a specific age

and the decisions that the person of a specific name

had to make

concerning the affordability of mustard and relish sandwiches at a specific age

when compared to other forms of nutrition

concerning the limited cost of mustard and relish sandwiches

because of their economic situation

when compared to other forms of nutrition

as it specifically pertains to the cost of food

because of their economic situation

because of the bankruptcy that the person of a specific name's mother

had to file for

as it specifically pertains to the cost of food

because of health coverage that the person of a specific name's

mother lost

because of the bankruptcy that the person of a specific

name's mother had to file for

because of the job that the person of a specific name's

mother lost

because of health coverage that the person of a specific name's mother lost

because of the days of work that the person of a specific name's mother

had to miss

because of the job that the person of a specific name's

mother lost

because of the tumour that was developing in the person

of a specific name's mother's body

because of the days of work that the person of a specific name's

mother had to miss

and how long it took the person of a specific name's mother's body to heal because of the tumour that was developing in the person of a specific

name's mother's body

and how long it took the person of a specific name's mother's

body to heal

and how the decisions that the person of a specific name

had to make at a specific age

concerning the affordability of mustard and relish sandwiches

when compared to other forms of nutrition

because of their economic situation

as it specifically pertains to the cost of food

because of the bankruptcy that the person of a specific name's

mother had to file for

because of health coverage that the person of a specific

name's mother lost

because of the job that the person of a specific name's mother lost

because of the days of work that the person of a specific name's mother

had to miss

because of the tumour that was developing in the person of a specific

name's mother's body

and how long it took the person of a specific name's

mother's body to heal

had inspired the person of a specific name

to work on your campaign specifically

this anecdote that you will end your speech with contains

another anecdote told by the person of a specific name

contained in the framing anecdote

who has had similar experiences to millions of other

young people in your specific nation

this anecdote that you will end your speech with contains

this anecdote that you will end your speech with contains

another anecdote told by the person of a specific name

another anecdote told by the person of a specific name

this anecdote that you will end your speech with contains

contained in the framing anecdote

contained in the framing anecdote

another anecdote told by the person of a specific name

this anecdote that you will end your speech with contains

and the decisions the person of a specific name made

contained in the framing anecdote

another anecdote told by the person of a specific name

this anecdote that you will end your speech with contains

regarding the person of a specific name's mother's situation

who could have made different decisions

contained in the framing anecdote

another anecdote told by the person of a specific name

this anecdote that you will end your speech with contains

based on the opinions of others

who could have made different decisions

contained in the framing anecdote

another anecdote told by the person of a specific name

based on the opinions of others

who could have made different decisions

contained in the framing anecdote

such as that one specific racial community is particularly lazy

based on the opinions of others

who could have made different decisions

such as that one specific racial community is particularly lazy

based on the opinions of others

or that members of another racial community are all illegal immigrants

such as that one specific racial
community is particularly lazy

or that members of another racial community are all illegal immigrants

but choose not to make decisions

based on those opinions

this anecdote that you will end your speech with contains

another anecdote told by the person of a specific name

contained in the framing anecdote

and the person of a specific name's decision

to build a coalition of people

from different specific communities

ii. on a high note

you have reached the end of your speech and you will finish your speech
with an anecdote the person of a specific name featured in the anecdote you
will finish your speech with has finished their anecdote the person of a
specific name featured in the anecdote you will finish your speech with
now asks others involved for their personal anecdotes the person of a
specific name featured in the anecdote you will finish your speech with
hears a variety of anecdotes the person of a specific name featured in the
anecdote you will finish your speech with hears also a variety of reasons to
support you the person of a specific name featured in the anecdote you will
finish your speech with hears a variety of specific issues the person of a
specific name featured in the anecdote you will finish your speech with
notices a person of no specific name the person of a specific name featured
in the anecdote you will finish your speech with notices a person of no
specific name and a broad age demographic the person of a specific name
featured in the anecdote you will finish your speech with notices a person

of no specific name and a broad age demographic and a specific racial identity the person of a specific name featured in the anecdote you will finish your speech with notices a person of no specific name and a broad age demographic and a specific racial identity who has yet to say a word the person of a specific name featured in the anecdote you will finish your speech with asks the person of no specific name and a broad age demographic and a specific racial identity who has yet to say a word why the person of no specific name and a broad age demographic and a specific racial identity who has yet to say a word is supporting your campaign for a specific office the person of no specific name and a broad age demographic and a specific racial identity who has yet to say a word does not describe any specific issue the person of no specific name and a broad age demographic and a specific racial identity who has yet to say a word does not say any specific medical issue the person of no specific name and a broad age demographic and a specific racial identity who has yet to say a word does not say any specific financial issue the person of no specific name and a broad age demographic and a specific racial identity who has yet to say a word does not say any specific issue regarding foreign conflict the person of no specific name and a broad age demographic and a specific racial identity who has yet to say a word does not say that the person of no specific name and a broad age demographic and a specific racial identity who has yet to say a word is not here because you are running for a specific office the person of no specific name and a broad age demographic and a specific racial identity who has yet to say a word say that they are here because of the person of a specific name and of a specific gender and of a specific age and of a specific race who works on your campaign for a specific office in a specific capacity in a specific city and primarily with a specific racial community for a specific amount of time who was asked why she was working on your campaign specifically among a group of other supporters of your noun for a specific office you have now reached the

end of the noun in which you will verb your speech with repeat the

answer given by the person of no specific name and adjective age

demographic and a specific adjective identity who has yet to say a noun

regarding the person of a specific name and of a specific gender and of a

specific age and of a specific race who works on pronoun campaign for a

specific office in a specific noun in a specific city and primarily with a specific racial community for a specific amount of time who was asked why

she was working on pronoun campaign specifically among a group of other

supporters of your campaign for a specific noun close your speech with

some relevant observational statements verb that this moment of

recognition between the person of a specific name and of a specific gender

and of a specific age and of a specific race who works on your campaign for

a specific office in a specific capacity in a specific noun and primarily with a

specific racial community for a specific amount of time who was asked why

they were working on your campaign specifically among a group of other

supporters of your campaign for a specific office and the person of no

specific name and a broad age demographic and a specific racial identity

who has yet to say a word is not enough to suggest that this moment of

noun between the person of a specific name and of a specific gender and of a specific age and of a specific race who works on your campaign for

office in a specific capacity in a specific city and primarily with a specific

racial community for a specific amount of noun who was asked why they

were working on your campaign specifically among a group of adjective

supporters of your campaign for a specific office and the noun of no

specific name and a broad age demographic and a specific racial identity

who has yet to verb a word is not enough to give people simple healthcare

suggest that this moment of recognition between the person of a specific

name and of a specific noun and of a specific age and of a specific race

who works on your campaign for office in a specific capacity in a specific

city and primarily with a specific racial community for a specific noun of

time who was asked conjunction they were working on your campaign

specifically among a group of other supporters of your campaign for a specific office and the person of adverb specific name and a broad age

demographic and a specific racial noun who has yet to say a word is not

enough to give people simple jobs suggest that this moment of recognition

between the person of a specific name and of a specific gender and of a

specific age and of a specific race who works on your campaign for office in

a specific capacity in a specific city and primarily with a specific racial

community for a specific amount of time who was asked why they were

working on your campaign specifically among a group of other plural noun

of your campaign for a specific office and the person of no specific name

and a broad age demographic and a specific racial noun who has yet to say a

word is not enough to give noun adjective education close your speech with

some more relevant observational statements suggest conjunction this noun

of recognition between the person preposition a specific name suggest that this moment of recognition and of a adjective gender between the person

of indefinite article specific name suggest that as an unspecific amount of

generations and of a specific age and of a specific gender have verb to

realize and of indefinite article adjective race and of a specific age over the

course of a specific amount of years who verb on your campaign for office

and of a specific noun since a particular group preposition people in a

specific capacity who works on pronoun campaign for office signed a

specific document in a specific city in a specific capacity in a specific noun

and primarily with a specific adjective community in a specific city that this

moment of recognition for a specific amount of noun and primarily with a specific racial noun between definite article person of a specific name who

was asked why plural pronoun were working on your campaign adverb for a

specific noun of time and of a specific gender preposition a group of other

supporters of your campaign who adverb asked why they were working on

your noun specifically and preposition a specific age for a specific office

among a group of adjective supporters of adjective campaign and of a

specific noun and the person of adverb specific name for a specific office

who works on your noun for office and a broad age noun and the person of

no specific noun in a specific capacity and a specific racial noun and a broad

age noun in a specific noun who has yet to say a noun and a specific racial noun and primarily with indefinite article specific racial noun is where we

start who has yet to say a word for a specific amount of time is where our

noun grows more adjective who was asked why they were working on

pronoun campaign specifically among a noun of other supporters of your

campaign for a specific office and the person of no adjective name and a

broad age demographic and a specific adjective identity who has yet to say a

noun is where perfection begins

[Applause]

you have reached the end of your speech

and the audience is applauding

you have reached the end of your speech

and you thank the audience very much

you have reached the end of your speech

and the audience is applauding

you have reached the end of your speech

and you thank the audience again

you have reached the end of your speech

and the audience is applauding

you have reached the end of your speech

and you thank the audience a third time

you have reached the end of your speech

and the audience is applauding

you have reached the end of your speech

and you walk off the stage

(July 2012)

[Acknowledgements]

Much like any great speech, a book of poetry is mothered by many.

My utmost thanks to Team BookThug. Jay MillAr and Hazel Millar are putting everything they have into an incredible ongoing project – one I'm so proud to be a part of. Thanks also to Rick Meier for all of his hard, hard work.

This text is greatly indebted to Charles Bernstein, who allowed himself to be implicated as the first editor of this project back in the summer of 2012. The incomparable Margaret Christakos gave me much to think about with a stimulating second reading. Andy Weaver helped plant the seeds for this text by introducing me to so much great work.

Portions of this poem have appeared in earlier incarnations since 2012. A version of "Begin Speech With" first appeared in the Summer 2012 issue of *The Puritan*, with thanks to editors Spencer Gordon and Mat Laporte. A version of "Contextualize Your Person" first appeared in the May 2013 issue of *Cough*, edited by David Peter Clark. Portions of "Understanding This Noun" first appeared in the Web Folio companion to the Spring 2014 issue of *The Capilano Review* and the uber-micro *HIJ* chapbook series in June of 2014; special thanks to Jenny Penberthy and Todd Nickel (*Capilano Review*), and Jay and Hazel (*HIJ*) respectively.

In October of 2013 Ferno House published a version of the first three sections of this poem as a chapbook entitled *Begin Speech With*. At that time, I would have put Ferno House's chapbooks against any in the English-speaking world. Spencer Gordon, Mat Laporte, Arnaud Brassard, and Patrick Larkin should all take a bow for the incredible run this micro-press had.

I am incredibly lucky to be surrounded by such an inspiring group of literary peers. Zoe Alexis Abrams, John Bell, Claire Caldwell, David Peter Clark, Spencer Gordon, Natalie Helberg, Liz Howard, Stevie Howell, Julie Joosten, Katie Jordon, Claire Lacey, Ben Ladouceur, Mat Laporte, Shannon Maguire, Sarah Pinder, Jenny Samparisi, Eric Schmaltz, Kilby Smith-McGregor, Fenn Stewart – thank you so much for your contributions and voices.

Special thanks to Kayla Matson, Shea Stewart, David Power, Adam Brady, Tom Hiley, and Whitney Hughes – all incredible people who have had to share a house with me as I either wrote or published this work, Kayla much longer than the rest.

Andrew Schwab for his great photos.

For their encouragement through this project: My mother Kathy, Seamus Atkinson, Dionne Brand, Lia Brewer, Rachel Brewer, Catherine Bush, Jasmyn Burke, Will Bustin, Candice Cassano, Joe Cressy, Bridgette Dalima, Craig Dodman, Rishma Dunlop, Margeaux Feldman, Nina Gorka, Kris Haig-Brown, Sally Headrick, Todd Hofley, Ralph Kolewe, The Layton – Chow family, Jessie Macaulay, Ausma Malik, Josh Mandryk, Sarah McLaughlin, Ramiro Mora, Evan Munday, Ted Nolan, Steve Nash, Edward Nixon, Ryna Olonan, Andrew Pulsifer, Zina Rita, Victoria Ryan, the Saunders – Dowdall family, Scotty and Hoffman, Emily Shelton, Mindi St. Amand, Meaghan Strimas, Marshall Tremblay, Kayla Turpin, and Alexandra Zampino.

[About the Author]

Jimmy McInnes was born and raised on Ontario's Bruce Peninsula. His first chapbook, *Begin Speech With*, was released by Ferno House in the fall of 2013. His poetry has appeared in various journals, including *This Magazine, ditch, The Puritan, Descant*, and the *Capilano Review Web Folio*. His work has been shortlisted for the Great Canadian Literary Hunt and the Robert Kroetsch Award for Innovative Poetry. He lives in Toronto, where he completed his MFA in Creative Writing at the University of Guelph, and is currently employed as a political hack. *A More Perfect [* is his first book-length work of poetry.

[Colophon]

Manufactured as the first edition of *A More Perfect [*
in the spring of 2015 by BookThug

Distributed in Canada by the Literary Press Group www.lpg.ca
Distributed in the USA by Small Press Distribution www.spdbooks.org

Shop online at www.bookthug.ca

BOOK
PRODUCTION
WAR ECONOMY
STANDARD

Type + design by Jay MillAr
Copy edited by Ruth Zuchter